Original title:
Searching for Meaning, but Forgot My Map

Copyright © 2025 Creative Arts Management OÜ
All rights reserved.

Author: Juliana Wentworth
ISBN HARDBACK: 978-1-80566-197-9
ISBN PAPERBACK: 978-1-80566-492-5

Lost in the Labyrinth of Thought

I wandered down a twisty lane,
With signs that made me feel insane.
The left was right, the up was down,
My thoughts a mix of joy and frown.

A signpost waved a cheery grin,
But which way leads me back again?
I asked a squirrel, lost in my plight,
He chattered back, 'You're quite the sight!'

Echoes of an Unwritten Journey

With a pen in hand, I'm set to roam,
But what's my plot? I'm far from home.
The pages blank, the ink runs dry,
I guess I'll wing it—oh my, oh my!

Each step I take, a comic scene,
A cast of characters, none routine.
I slip on dreams, I trip on fate,
And hope the end will come not late.

The Compass of the Heart

I pulled out my heart, a compass wise,
But it spun around, oh what a surprise!
It pointed north, then south with glee,
I think it's laughing more than me!

With each direction leading astray,
I'm fine with chaos, come what may.
I'll dance in circles, skip through the mess,
For joy's the compass, I must confess!

Navigating with Blindfolded Eyes

A blindfold snug, I walked with flair,
Bumping into walls, but I don't care.
With giggles echoing, I feel alive,
Who needs to see when you can jive?

Each step a mystery, a twist of fate,
With laughter leading, oh isn't it great?
I'll stumble, tumble, and make a scene,
In this grand maze, I'm a dancing queen!

Charting a Course through Shadows

The compass spins like a top,
I chase the sun, it decides to drop.
With stars as guides, but none to trust,
I trip on clouds, oh what a bust!

A map of giggles, lines go askew,
In a forest of questions, where am I to?
The trees just chuckle, their leaves a cheer,
But I can't find my way, oh dear, oh dear!

The Puzzle Beneath the Surface

Pieces scattered, where do I fit?
Jigsaw blues, I'm losing it!
A corner here, a side there,
But where's the edge? I pull my hair!

With every twist, a laugh erupts,
I ask the cat—she just erupts.
She ponders deeply, then swats a piece,
And I'm reminded of my lack of peace.

Where the Wild Questions Roam

In the fields of ponder, wild thoughts soar,
Are ducks just swans that fell on the floor?
With every question, I lose my track,
The answers scatter, then swiftly snack!

I wander through laughs, questions like sheep,
Some jump the fence, oh what a leap!
With every laugh, uncertainty blends,
But that's the fun—where it all transcends!

The Silence of Inconclusive Roads

I wander paths that lead nowhere,
Each branch a riddle, an empty stare.
The signs all point, but none agree,
I ponder, 'Is the joke on me?'

A chuckle echoes through trees so dense,
As I try to reason with pure suspense.
With every stride, I dance with doubt,
The journey's the punchline; I laugh it out!

The Signposts of Yesterday

Where did I leave my trusty guide?
A squirrel stole it, I can't decide.
Maps in my pocket, or so I thought,
But a duck quacked loudly; I'm now distraught.

The signs point to pizza, but I want the sea,
Why does every turn look just like a tree?
A compass spins round, like a dancer in flight,
I'll follow the breadcrumbs, they're my best light.

Beneath the Weight of Untraveled Roads

With snacks in my bag, I venture anew,
But GPS says, 'Who are you to pursue?'
I hit a fork, and it looks quite grim,
Should I follow the cat, or the crow with a whim?

My shoes are too tight, and my head's in a daze,
Why did I think I could navigate mazes?
Oh look, a treasure! Wait, it's just mold!
I'll trade it for laughter; let's break the fold.

In Search of Lost Horizons

I packed up my dreams, all shiny and bright,
Then tripped over thoughts in the middle of night.
A rainbow appeared, then it vanished so fast,
Is it just in my head, or reflected from glass?

With socks on my hands, I'm caught in a jam,
I'll just wing it, like a confused little lamb.
The sky is a canvas, but I brought a broom,
Now I'm painting my way to a sunlit room.

The Road Less Taken

Two paths diverged in a crowded café,
One leads to coffee, the other a stray.
I'll take the one that smells like burnt bread,
While dreams of a pastry dance in my head.

Around every corner, my thoughts start to play,
A fiddle with mishaps, come what may.
But a clown on a unicycle steals my attention,
And off I go, sans any intention.

Scribbles on the Fabric of Time

In the attic, dust collects,
Lost stories old and new.
Markings on a crumpled sheet,
A treasure map for fools like you.

Coffee stains on midnight thoughts,
Show me where I left my keys.
A battle lost to socks and dreams,
My mind's a puzzle with no fees.

Chasing shadows, dodging light,
With only breadcrumbs for a guide.
The cat's my compass, purrs at night,
Directing me to pizza's side.

Yet laughter bursts from messed-up paths,
With each detour, joy expands.
Forget the route, let's share some laughs,
In this wild journey, take my hand.

A Wanderer's Notebook

With crayon sketches of my dreams,
A jigsaw puzzle made of foam.
I scribble down these wild extremes,
While chasing clouds I've yet to own.

My shoelaces dance in perfect sync,
To melodies I can't define.
Each corner turned, another blink,
Where chaos and discovery entwine.

Through candy streets and popcorn skies,
I juggle hopes like flaming pies.
Each falter's just a chance to rise,
As laughter echoes where truth lies.

In margins wide, the secrets sprout,
A doodle here, a dream shown out.
Life's an art, no need for doubt,
Let's trip through worlds that twist about.

The Intrigue of Curved Lines

Curvy roads and crooked signs,
Invite me to a dance of ways.
With left turns leading, oh so fine,
And right spins bringing endless plays.

Maps have vanished in the fun,
Yet laughter maps my every turn.
Let's pitch our tents beneath the sun,
While silly accidents we learn.

I bought a load of mystery snacks,
Unraveled tales in every bite.
With chocolate whispers, giggles crack,
A feast of chaos, pure delight!

With crayons as my chosen tools,
I sketch the world with one-eyed grace.
Each wobbly footstep breaks the rules,
On this endless, wild goose chase.

The Beauty in Uncharted Terrain

A wanderer on paths unknown,
With pockets full of hopes and cheer.
I dance where flowers have overgrown,
With wild heights to disappear.

Navigating through the silly sighs,
With giggles trailing in my wake.
A compass lost, but what's a prize?
When clumsy rhythms start to break.

The clouds are sticky, like my hair,
As thoughts become a jumble stew.
I draw new maps with flair and dare,
For every wrong turn brings me you.

In this maze of muddled grace,
We celebrate each silly twist.
With coffee spills, and ginger pacing,
Let's find the joy that can't be missed.

Cartography of the Heart

In a land where X marks the spot,
Love's compass spins, and I'm in a knot.
With no directions, I wander so free,
Lost in my thoughts, like a runaway bee.

Google Maps failed, how can this be?
Marked 'Do Not Enter' but beckons to me.
Drawn to the places I swore I would flee,
My heart leads me here, 'Come dance with me!'

A Journey Through the Mist

Fog envelops all paths that I take,
Muffled laughter blooms, make no mistake.
With a map made of candy, I feel like a fool,
Stepping on gum, adherence to rule.

The landmarks are blurry, but isn't that fun?
One's a bear, and the other—a bun!
Through giggles and stumbles, I skirt the surprise,
Who knew meaning's a haze, adorned with pink skies?

The Map to Nowhere

This cryptic scroll claims treasures await,
Scribbled in crayon, a wild, wild fate.
With every direction, I'm going askew,
But pizza's ahead, a delicious debut!

I turn left for laughter, then right for pie.
In these wanderings, I can't help but sigh.
Nowhere feels closer when food's on my plate,
So let's toss the map and just celebrate!

Uncharted Waters of the Soul

Sailing a ship with no anchor or sail,
My heart's a balloon, afloat without trail.
With each wave I ride, I laugh at the view,
Why find a harbored truth? I'll just paddle through!

My compass is broken, but the sea's always bright,
With jellyfish waltzing and seagulls in flight.
No map in the water, yet I float with glee,
In these uncharted depths, I am totally me!

In the Footsteps of Forgotten Heroes

In a realm where legends sleep,
I wander trails too wide and steep.
With my trusty snack in hand,
I search for wisdom in this land.

The capes I wear are slightly tattered,
But fashion's not what ever mattered.
I asked a squirrel for advice,
He just stared back, not so nice!

Each rock I trip on tells a tale,
Of valiant knights who'd never fail.
It's hard to find those missing maps,
When every corner leads to naps.

Yet laughter is my compass true,
As I stroll this path anew.
Heroes lost but joy remains,
In silly walks and random gains.

Roads Diverged in Twilight

Two paths before me twist and bend,
One smells like bread, the other, a blend.
Do I follow my nose or my gut?
Decisions made, but I'm still in a rut.

A talking frog hops by my side,
Saying, 'Choose wisely, there's no need to hide!'
But why should I heed a frog's advice,
When he's just here for the gravy rice?

I juggle signs like a circus clown,
While pondering which way to get down.
Do I risk a trip through the brambles,
Or take the route with the prancing ramblers?

In twilight glow, I laugh too loud,
As confusion wraps me like a shroud.
For every step holds laughs, not fear,
And maybe that's the map right here!

The Canvas of the Unseen Journey

I'm painting paths with colors bright,
Mixing joy with a hint of fright.
Each stroke a journey, wild and free,
But where the canvas ends, who will see?

I toss my paint, it splatters wide,
Like my brain when I've tried to decide.
A purple llama, a green tree house,
This art's a mess, just like the mouse!

My easel shakes, what's the next hue?
Do I paint success or the things I rue?
With every dab, I giggle and snort,
As I sketch my way to a whimsical court.

Here's to abstracts and odd designs,
For meaning hides within fine lines.
Embracing chaos, laughing at fate,
This canvas cheers me to celebrate!

Unfolding the Secrets of the Universe

In search of answers, I grab my spoon,
To eat the cosmos under the moon.
With cereal stars and milk of dreams,
I ponder life's perplexing themes.

Gravity's a prankster, pulls me down,
While I'm just trying to twirl around.
I asked a comet for some clues,
But all it gave was cosmic blues!

Black holes make for charming jokes,
As even the wise say, 'It pokes and pokes.'
The secrets swirl in a dance so grand,
I chase them like a lost rubber band.

So here I stand with my goofy grin,
As stars and giggles around me spin.
Unfolding laughter, what's the rush?
In this universe, let's create a hush!

A Tapestry of Question Marks

In a jungle of doubt, I wander,
With no signposts or clues for ponder.
My compass spins in dizzy delight,
A treasure map? No, just a kite.

I trip on shoelaces of thought,
While pondering what I haven't sought.
The squirrels laugh, they know the game,
As I haphazardly keep forgetting my name.

With a backpack full of chaotically bright gear,
I trip, I tumble, I chuckle, I cheer.
The peanut gallery of clouds all conspire,
To send me off on a quest to nowhere higher.

A quest for wisdom, mislaid like my hat,
But every step is a chortle and that's where it's at.
In a tapestry woven with giggles and quirks,
I'm lost but it's jolly, amidst all my jerks.

The Echo of Distant Landscapes

Bouncing echoes of thoughts on a loop,
Like a clumsy kangaroo doing the hoop.
I shout out queries into the thick air,
And they bounce back giggling, oh, they dare!

With every curve in this unruly road,
A snail's pace seems like quite the load.
I chase down shadows with whimsical grace,
While dodging the gazes of bewildered space.

I follow breadcrumbs made of bright jokes,
As owls roll their eyes at bumbling blokes.
The landscape shifts with a wink and a grin,
As my imaginary map looks a bit thin.

Yet here I stand, with a laugh in my chest,
Unraveling riddles, forsaking the quest.
In echoing valleys, my laughter's the trace,
Of a journey so silly, I'd never replace.

Through the Fog of Misguided Paths

Through the misty haze, I fumble and trip,
Wearing mismatched socks and a banana chip.
Questions float like balloons in the breeze,
While I dance with confusion beneath the trees.

Each branch whispers secrets, riddles so deep,
But the answers are just playing hide and seek.
A squirrel gives directions with a spin and a twist,
Yet all I can see is a very foggy mist.

I toss a coin to the winds of chance,
Expecting some wisdom, but they just prance.
"Lost?" they chuckle, "Oh, join the fun!"
And my map? It just might be another pun.

With every wrong turn, I add to the tale,
Turning my misadventures into a sale.
Through fog and folly, chuckling loud,
In this silly maze, I'm warmly enshrouded.

A Universe of Unanswered Queries

In a cosmos where questions abound,
I float like a balloon, lost, but unbound.
Stars twinkle like giggles, bright in the night,
But what does it mean? Oh, just takes flight.

I sailed on a comet wearing mismatched shoes,
While Saturn and Mars mocked my clueless blues.
"Hey, look at him!" they snicker and jeer,
As I draft up a letter to my forgotten sphere.

With a quill made of stardust and a heart full of glee,
I scribble in circles, wondering, "What's free?"
But the universe winks, like a wise old sage,
And dances around on an infinite stage.

In this whimsical void of questions galore,
I laugh with the planets, not seeking much more.
For among the uncertainties, laughter's the key,
In a universe sprawling, so grand and so free.

A Heart Without a Guidebook

I walked the path with socks askew,
The sun was bright, but I had no clue.
I followed squirrels and rogue balloons,
Chasing dreams beneath cartoon moons.

Each signpost laughed, I swear they grinned,
Points to nowhere, where to begin?
With every turn, I lost my way,
And made a game of dismay each day.

A map would help, but it feels like a prank,
My heart's the compass, but it's drawing blanks.
So here I go, on this wild spree,
A treasure hunt with no X to see.

But who needs maps when laughs abound?
With every stumble, joy is found.
In this adventure, I might get lost,
But giggles are worth whatever the cost.

Whispers of the Wind

The breeze told tales of times to come,
But I just danced and let out a hum.
With every gust, I felt a push,
Yet tripped on leaves with a dizzy whoosh.

I chased a kite, it led me astray,
While pigeons cooed like they knew the way.
The world was wise, or so they swore,
But I just wanted to find a store.

The wind would whisper, "Find your truth!"
While I stood still, clutching my tooth.
With puzzled frowns and silly grins,
I rode the current, where laughter wins.

With every twist the jokes grow stout,
In this wacky whirl, life's what it's about.
So if there's wisdom in the air,
It's best enjoyed with a debonair flair.

The Crossroads of Doubt

At the crossroads, I scratched my head,
One way to comfort, the other to dread.
A sign marked 'Wisdom' was out of sight,
While another said, 'Dare to take flight!'

I stood and pondered, which route to tread?
One road had snacks, the other had bread.
Twisting and turning, it felt like a game,
Every choice I made felt oddly the same.

The trees looked down, gave a knowing wink,
As I pondered hard, I started to blink.
Should I turn left for a dance with fate,
Or right for a nap, I think I'll be late.

In this jungle of thought and mirth,
Laughter echoes, my best friend on earth.
Turns out, it's a laugh to dwell on doubt,
In the crossroads, it's the giggle that counts.

Unraveled Threads of Destiny

With threads of fate tangled around,
Lost in fabric, I fell to the ground.
Each stitch a joke, each knot a plan,
But my sewing skills? Oh, where'd they ran?

A tapestry bright with colors so bold,
Unraveling tales of the goofy and old.
I tugged and pulled at the seams of fate,
And all I got was a laggard gait.

"Who needs a tailor?" I boldly proclaimed,
As I wandered forth, slightly ashamed.
The threads of life danced in the breeze,
Tickling my sides and bringing me to my knees.

So here I am, a patchwork of glee,
With every fray, I find my spree.
In this messy weave, I stumble and trip,
But laugh till I cry on this adventure trip.

Wandering Through the Mist of Uncertainty

Lost among clouds, I trip on air,
My compass laughs, it seems unfair.
I chase the sun, it runs too fast,
While puddles of doubt form shadows cast.

The trees giggle, they shake with glee,
A squirrel offers advice for free.
Yet where to go, I'm still unclear,
Maybe just dance, that's what I hear!

Maps of Memory

I drew a map from dreams long past,
But it seems my lines were drawn too fast.
There's an 'X' where my lunch should be,
And arrows pointing back to me!

I ask a toaster for directions,
It pops up bread with great affection.
A paperclip leads me on a spree,
To find my keys? Now that's the key!

Streets of Dreams

I stroll down avenues of thought,
Where every sign says, 'Give it a shot!'
The traffic lights flash, but it's all a blur,
A talking dog offers me a fur.

In alleys of whimsy, I lose my way,
Laughter echoes at the end of play.
On the corner has-beens sell ice cream cones,
With flavors named after forgotten phones!

The Trail of Unanswered Questions

Each step I take leads to a chat,
With rocks that ponder where I'm at.
The bushes giggle, 'Is this your quest?'
I shrug and wonder who knows best.

Clouds overhead play peek-a-boo,
While ducks debate the skies of blue.
I ask the wind, it just blows by,
With a wink, it says, 'No need to try!'

In Pursuit of the Whispering Horizon

The horizon whispers secrets sweet,
But it's miles away on this bumpy street.
With every step, a new giggle blooms,
Balloons float by like tiny costumes.

Sunsets tease me with shades of gold,
Yet the view ahead is ever bold.
I'll chase the dawn, with no regret,
As shadows dance, I forget the fret!

Sailing Beyond Familiar Shores

I set sail with a sock for a guide,
The stars laughed at my reckless pride.
Waves danced with intuitive flair,
A seagull squawked, 'Do you even care?'

The compass spun like a playful spin,
I hooted, 'Adventure! Let the fun begin!'
Bumping into islands made of cheese,
And here I thought, 'This could be a tease.'

Echoes of What Was Left Behind

I tripped over echoes of forgotten lore,
Spilling secrets on the sandy floor.
Where did I leave my sunglasses bright?
Oh wait, they're cookin' in the sunlight.

The sandcastle fell, a majestic grief,
Crowded by crabs, my nemesis, the chief.
They whispered tales of my blundering fate,
I nodded, thinking, 'This was first-rate!'

Beyond the Horizon of Remembered Dreams

I followed clouds that looked like cake,
But all I found was a mighty lake.
Ducks quacked loudly, mocking my plan,
'You really thought you'd outrun the man?'

I chased a rainbow, a slippery sprite,
Hoping to catch it, much to my plight.
But all they gave me were giggles and glares,
Reminding me I should've checked my layers.

Verses Written in the Void

In a void where doodles chose to play,
I scribbled nonsense throughout the day.
Each line a treasure lost in the mist,
With thoughts so jumbled, you get the gist.

The ink was spilled, a colorful mess,
Hoping, somehow, it might impress.
Yet all I got was a dance-off with fate,
Turns out, my moves were best left to wait.

The Quest for Stars Beneath My Feet

With a compass that spins like it's lost its mind,
I wander the fields, hoping stars I can find.
Each step leads me where puddles reflect,
Not quite the night sky, but hey, it's a trek!

A map made of jelly? Now that's a fine joke,
I slip and I slide, oh what a wild poke!
The grass whispers secrets, the flowers all laugh,
Yet here I am, stuck in my own silly gaffe.

I ask passing squirrels for wisdom so grand,
They just chatter back, hardly a helping hand.
With each goofy tumble, I lose track of time,
But the giggles around me feel just so sublime.

So here I shall dance, with no set direction,
Rediscovering joy in this quirky collection.
Though stars may elude me, they're close to my heart,
In the search for the laughs, I've already found art.

Echoes of the Unwritten Path

In the wild of my thoughts, I leap and I bound,
With every odd twist, I feel wisdom surround.
The breadcrumbs I drop are more like a feast,
A buffet of nonsense, at least not the least!

I follow my shadow, it's quite full of sass,
It rolls its own eyes as I stumble on grass.
Oh, where is the trail? It keeps switching its name,
Like a game of charades; it's all just the same.

A kite in the wind says, 'let's have some fun!'
While I trip over roots trying to catch me a sun.
Each laugh that I echo rings loud in the air,
Turns this strange journey into one full of flair.

With no written guide, it feels so absurd,
But every step taken brings joy that's unheard.
So onward I wander, with giggles as my map,
And who knew sweet nonsense was the best kind of clap?

Navigating the Sea of Doubt

I sail on a ship made of bubblegum dreams,
Navigating waters that swirl with strange beams.
The stars are my crew, they twinkle and jest,
As I paddle along, they say, 'You're the best!'

The waves try to toss me, oh what a big joke,
A fish with a hat says 'Hey, can I poke?'
I laugh as I bob like a cork in the tide,
These silly distractions keep me bona fide.

Old anchors of worry drag deep in the sea,
But I trade them for jellyfish dancing with glee.
Oh, what have I found in this ocean so bright?
A treasure of folly, bathed in pure light!

So I sail on, laughing, with each silly twist,
For even the storms can't dampen my bliss.
In this sea of confusion, I'll anchor my heart,
For every wave carries wisdom, a brand new smart start.

Fragments of a Forgotten Road

On a road made of giggles and sparkles, I roam,
With signs that say 'Left!' but I'm sure it's just foam.
I trip over jokes that are lying around,
Like banana peels scattered on this goofy ground.

A backpack of whimsy weighs down on my back,
Full of glitter and mishaps, oh, what a whack!
Each step into nonsense, a riddle to crack,
I'm mapping my future, but can't find the track.

A dog wearing glasses barks wisdom in barks,
But I swear he's just barking at cat-shaped parks.
I chuckle and listen to the stories they weave,
As breadcrumbs of laughter lead to what I believe.

So here I shall wander, a jester in bloom,
With fragments of paths spun around in my room.
Though maps may elude me, I cherish the ride,
For in this strange journey, my joys are my guide.

The Mapmaker's Lament

I drew a map of dreams so bright,
But found it led me to the right.
With every twist and turn I took,
I ended up in someone's nook.

The X marks spots I thought I knew,
Turned out to be a silly zoo.
I asked a llama where to go,
It laughed and said, "Just take it slow!"

I packed my bags for lands unknown,
Only to find I'd lost my phone.
A compass broke, my plans went south,
I followed breadcrumbs straight to mouth.

Now wandering brings me fits of glee,
As I cavort with squirrels and tea.
In misadventure, laughs abound,
Who needs a map when joy is found?

Journeying Through the Void

In the void where stars don't shine,
I stumbled over cosmic wine.
I juggled planets, lost my way,
A black hole pulled me in to play.

With comets whizzing past my head,
I ponder why I got out of bed.
An alien asked for directions,
I pointed left, gave wrong reflections.

Through shooting stars, I zigged and zagged,
My GPS just laughed and bragged.
My spaceship's now a disco ball,
A dance-off's how I made the call.

So here's to space with all its charms,
Where I can twirl in zero arms.
No route prescribed for me to roam,
In this void, I've found my home!

Chasing Fireflies in the Dark

In twilight hues, I chase the light,
While tripping under stars so bright.
With jars in hand and laughter free,
I'm catching dreams, not meant to be.

A firefly flits just out of reach,
I stagger onward, like at beach.
But in the dark, I fumble around,
And bump my head on grassy ground.

The night is filled with twinkling sparks,
As I perform my silly larks.
Each glow I catch, a fleeting friend,
Yet still I search where shadows bend.

But as the dawn begins to rise,
I laugh at all my silly tries.
In mischief's glow, I've lost my aim,
But joy is found in this sweet game!

Dreams Carved in Starry Dust

With dreams that twinkle in the night,
I carved my path with sheer delight.
Yet every turn was full of fun,
Like stumbling when I meant to run.

The stars all giggled in a line,
As I insisted I was fine.
A shooting star said, "Wanna race?"
But tripped over the cosmic lace.

In swirling dust, my plans went haywire,
I tangoed with a cosmic choir.
Each note a wish that I once shared,
Yet here I am, totally unprepared.

So let the universe conspire,
With dreams that twinkle and inspire.
In starry dreams, we laugh and play,
Forget the map, it's a fun-filled day!

Eclipsed Journeys and Undefined Destinies

In shadows deep, I roam and stray,
With friends asleep, I lost my way.
I hitched a ride on a bumblebee,
It buzzed so loud, it set me free.

With mismatched socks and a crooked grin,
I followed a squirrel, thought it was kin.
It led me to a fountain that sputtered,
And there my worries, they just fluttered.

Maps are for those who plan ahead,
I just seek coffee and a warm bed.
A taco stand under the starry night,
That's the compass, it feels so right.

So here I stand, with pastries galore,
My trail's a mystery, but who keeps score?
In every wrong turn, a giggle I've found,
These eclipsed journeys are joyfully profound.

Meadows of Uncertainty

Wandering through fields where daisies play,
I tripped on thoughts that led me astray.
The sun's a clown, it juggles the light,
While I lose my steps, but feel alright.

Grass stains on my pants, what a sight,
I followed a butterfly, oh what a flight!
With every gust, my hat took a leap,
Now it's off with the clouds, flying cheap.

I packed a sandwich that's squished and small,
In meadows of doubt, I still stand tall.
A dance with the weeds, a game that I play,
In this wacky world, I'll find my way.

So let the wind guide, let laughter unwind,
In quirky places, all treasures I find.
With each little mishap, a chuckle I glean,
In meadows so wild, I reign like a queen.

The Heartbeat of the Untraveled

I've got no map, just a heart that's bold,
With pockets of wishes and stories untold.
I followed a pigeon, it seemed to know,
It took a wrong turn, as pigeons do so.

My compass spins like a topsy toy,
Chasing each laugh, oh what a joy!
The sidewalk sings with each hop I take,
In the grumbles of doubt, I still feel awake.

With quirky thoughts that dance in my head,
I stumble on pathways of pink jelly spread.
The pulse of adventure, it beats in my chest,
Each clumsy misstep is just like a jest.

So here's to the paths that twist and bend,
In the heartbeat of travel, I find a friend.
With humor and whimsy, I skip through the scene,
In this untraveled life, I'm forever a dream.

Lanterns in an Unmapped Forest

In woods so thick, where shadows dance,
I tripped on roots, oh what a chance!
A lantern glows, but it's just a glowworm,
Leading me on, while my thoughts squirm.

The trees are wise, they whisper and tease,
I ask for direction, they just say, 'Please!'
With branches that tickle and vines that entwine,
I follow the light, as I sip on moonshine.

I chased a raccoon as it rummaged with glee,
It winked at me, how charmingly free!
The forest giggles, it knows my plight,
In this uncharted territory, I'll be alright.

So let's light a path with laughter and song,
In lantern-lit woods where I belong.
With every wrong turn, there's fun to be found,
In this unmapped forest, my joy knows no bound.

Serendipity in a Sea of Chaos

Woke up today, lost my way,
Feels like a game I forgot to play.
Coffee spills on my old map,
Guess I'm just a wandering chap.

I trip on laughter, bump into fate,
Every wrong turn feels first-rate.
Found a cat, it looks quite wise,
Gave me directions to the skies.

Pursuing paths that twist and twine,
Dancing with shadows, sipping brine.
Birds sing secrets, grass tickles feet,
Who knew confusion could be so sweet?

With every step, I spin and twirl,
Caught in a whirl of a dizzying swirl.
Maps are overrated, or so I hear,
I'll take this chaos, have no fear!

Searching for Signposts in the Void

I'm lost on this road, it's quite absurd,
Could use a sign or just one word.
Doodles in the dust, a laugh or two,
I guess I'll follow where the pigeons flew.

Every turn I make, it's quite divine,
Chasing clouds, I'm sipping wine.
Who needs a compass to find their way?
Just watch the squirrels, they'll lead the play.

With each misstep, I gain some grace,
A tumble here, a giggle at pace.
Balloons float past, no strings attached,
Life's a party and I'm quite mismatched.

Nowhere to go, yet everywhere to roam,
I'll dance in circles, make it my home.
Maps are for those who play it safe,
I'd rather ride the silliness wave!

A Map Written in the Stars

Stars overhead, they wink and wink,
Feels like a cosmic game, don't you think?
I squint my eyes at the patterns up high,
What do they mean? Oh me, oh my!

Constellations point to dinner tonight,
Or maybe a dance under moonlight bright.
I'll follow the glow of a neon sign,
Where chaos and cupcakes intertwine.

Planets align, but I've lost my way,
Chasing fireworks in the light of day.
Astrological clues lead me astray,
But I laugh as I prance, come what may.

With glittering dreams up in the sky,
I'll sketch my path, I won't be shy.
Who needs a map when skies ignite?
Let's wave to the stars, dance in their light!

In the Quiet of Uncertainty

In the silence, confusion reigns,
I trip on thoughts like scattered grains.
Should I wear socks with sandals today?
Embrace the oddness, come what may!

A whisper of doubt tickles my ear,
Yet silly antics make everything clear.
I laugh at riddles spun in my head,
Maybe I'll dance on a slice of bread.

Sometimes I stumble, but oh what fun,
A tumble, a roll, and then I run.
In this ruckus, I find my cheer,
Lost in translation, yet perfectly here.

So here's to the joy in twists and turns,
A light-hearted heart that forever yearns.
Maps may elude, but I've found my part,
In the quiet of chaos, I feel my heart!

Footprints on the Sands of Doubt

In the sand I left my shoes,
Hoping for wisdom, I found a bruise.
The tide rolled in, it washed away,
My footprints laughed, 'You lost your way!'

With every step, I looked around,
A crab approached, it made no sound.
I asked it, 'Hey, which way to go?'
It blinked at me, 'I don't know, bro!'

I tried to follow a seagull's squawk,
But it flapped off, leaving a mock.
The shells I gathered meant nothing at all,
Just pointed me back, towards the mall!

Perhaps a compass can fix this mess,
But all I have is this silly dress.
I'll dance along this sandy track,
In the end, it's just the fun that I'll pack!

The Inkwell of Lost Directions

My pen dipped deep in an inkwell's seam,
I penned my fate, or so it would seem.
Each stroke a risk, each word a quest,
Yet letters tangled, I couldn't rest.

The map I drew was full of bends,
Each path I charted led to dead ends.
I scribbled 'North' though I faced the sun,
And laughed aloud because this was fun!

A pirate's treasure, I sought in vain,
But all I found was a rubber chicken's reign.
It danced and clucked, a fine delight,
Maybe I'm lost, but I'll be alright.

As ink ran dry, my thoughts took flight,
I discovered joy in my inky plight.
So here I am, a poet of cheer,
With each silly twist, I hold you dear!

Querying the Stars in a Clouded Sky

I aimed my gaze at the night so bright,
But clouds conspired to block my sight.
I asked each star, 'Do you have a clue?'
They winked and laughed, 'Not from this view!'

With telescope broken, I squinted and begged,
For answers wrapped up in cosmic dread.
I pulled out a guide, but it turned to dust,
In the mysteries of space, I just must trust.

A comet streamed by, all flashy and bold,
I yelled, 'Hey you, have you been told?'
It shot past so fast, said, 'Catch me if you can!'
But I tripped on my dreams, along with the plan.

As meteors fell with a splash and a pop,
I gathered them up, hoping they'd stop.
A cosmic giggle echoed through the night,
Maybe being lost means feeling just right!

The Pilgrim's Paradox

With a walking stick and shoes untied,
I marched forth, full of misplaced pride.
Chasing the horizon with no map in hand,
My list of goals was not quite grand.

I asked a goat for wisdom, you see,
It just chewed grass and looked back at me.
A sassy bird chirped, 'You silly lad!'
Seems even the animals thought it was bad!

Through thickets and thorns, I stumbled around,
All the while, fooling myself I was profound.
I dropped my snack in a puddle of mud,
Yet laughter erupted, as I stood with a thud!

By the campfire's glow, my friends gathered 'round,
With stories and snacks, no need for profound.
In this merry mess, what I truly learned,
Is that joy is the map and my heart is unturned!

Threads of Intuition in a Tangled Web

In a world where whispers dance,
I lost my way, without a chance.
Maps were drawn in crayon bold,
Funny tales now left untold.

I followed breadcrumbs just for fun,
Wound up chasing my own spun.
The signs were clear, or so they said,
But my GPS is out of red.

I stumbled upon a zany crew,
Who offered tea and bags of goo.
Together we lost track of time,
Dancing well past the dull rhyme.

Now I wander with silly glee,
In my pocket, a mystery.
With laughter loud and joy unscripted,
My path may be strange, yet it's encrypted.

Beneath the Veil of Illusions

Beneath the guise of morning dew,
I wear a hat that's slightly askew.
I seek the truth in coffee grounds,
Yet all I find are joyful sounds.

A knight mistook my floppy shoe,
Claimed it a sign, he'd follow too!
So onward we trod, a merry band,
With a roadmap drawn in shifting sand.

We stumbled o'er the garden hedge,
Found ourselves upon a ledge.
Where was the path I thought I'd charted?
Turns out all leave me, quite outsmarted.

Now I wear a cloak of glee,
As squirrels whisper ancient mystery.
Through humorous flops, I find delight,
In each weird turn, my heart takes flight.

Through the Fog, a Flicker of Insight

Through the fog of whims and wishes,
I often trip in muddy dishes.
With a flashlight from last year's Halloween,
I chase the glow, unsure and green.

A sock puppet gave me sage advice,
"Life's a game, just roll the dice!"
So I laughed and tossed my cares,
While waltzing through invisible snares.

Clouds of doubt clouded my view,
Yet I danced with every clue.
An acorn fell, a gentle nudge,
Said, "Just move on, don't hold a grudge!"

So I pirouetted past confusion,
With twirls that bled into illusion.
Through silly mishaps I find my way,
Wit and joy my guide each day.

The Untraveled Path of the Soul

On a path less trodden, I did roam,
With mismatched shoes, I called it home.
I stumbled, skipped, and fell on rocks,
Chasing shadows in silly socks.

A fortune teller said, "You'll find,"
A treasure that's both sweet and kind.
I smiled and laughed while sipping tea,
For the treasure, you see, is just me.

Past the bushes that whisper loud,
I danced like a happy crowd.
The road was bent like a silly straw,
Yet it's the laughter I adore.

Now I skip through life's quirky game,
Chasing joy without the shame.
Each stumble brings a giggle or two,
And who needs a map, when you're so true?

When Directions Fade Away

I packed my bag with snacks and zest,
But left my map and that's a jest.
With every turn, I'm more perplexed,
I'm starting to question what comes next.

The signs are blurry, the roads all twist,
I've lost my way, it's quite the tryst.
A friendly bird just chirped and laughed,
I guess I'm on the wrong path, by half.

My GPS is now a joke,
It leads me where the wild things poke.
I pass a cow that gives a stare,
As if to say, 'Are you going somewhere?'

Through fields of clover, I stumble and sway,
Is this the road to good ol' Café?
I'll grab a treat, forget the route,
Sometimes a donut's what it's all about.

Footprints in the Sand of Memory

In grains of time, my steps are spun,
My feet in sand, or maybe just fun.
I hold a starfish, a jester's friend,
What was I looking for again, to mend?

The tide rolls in with a salty grin,
It washes away what I thought was kin.
A crab waves 'hi', with his pincers wide,
He knows this beach, I'm the one that's tried.

The seagulls squawk, they're in a row,
They've got a map, but I'm just slow.
I build a castle, oh what a fool,
Who needs a map when you have a pool?

With shells like treasures, I fill my sack,
But still can't find my way back.
A beach ball bounces, it steals my chase,
I guess I'll just wander in this sunny place.

Shadows of a Vanished Guide

Once I had a guide with a booming voice,
But now I'm left to make my own choice.
I trust my feet, but they lead astray,
Now I'm more lost than a cat in a play.

The shadows dance, they lead the way,
With twists and turns that boldly sway.
I ask a llama where I should go,
It shrugs, and off the cliff I almost flow.

A rabbit hops with a knowing gleam,
He winks at me like it's a dream.
I follow him, to a party, what fun!
But did I mention, I forgot the sun?

With confetti falling like shredded maps,
I laugh at life's very tricky traps.
Turns out the journey ends in cheer,
Just don't ask me where I'll wander near.

The Veil of Uncertainty

A fog rolls in, like a thick wool sweater,
I seek the path, but it's getting wetter.
With every step, I question my luck,
My compass spins—oh, what the ... ?

I trip on thoughts that float like mist,
Each whisper tells me something's amiss.
A squirrel in glasses shakes his head,
"You'll need a map, or a trusty thread!"

Beneath the veil, I dance and swerve,
Do I follow this path, do I need to conserve?
The trees are gossiping, quite a chatter,
While I try to decipher what's really the matter.

But laughter hides in the folds of doubt,
Embracing chaos, I twirl about.
In confusion's embrace, I'll take a stand,
Who needs a plan when you've got a band?

The Search for the Hidden Key

In a jacket pocket, I found a sock,
Could it be the key, or just a block?
I turned it upside down, gave it a shake,
Hoping for answers, just this once, for my sake.

I tried the fridge and checked the floor,
A quest for wisdom, but found a whores.
A cat gave me sass, a dog looked confused,
As I scratched my head, feeling widely amused.

I climbed a tree, my head in a fog,
I looked for insights, but found just a dog.
He wagged his tail, said, 'Chill, relax!'
While I felt the weight of my missing tracks.

In the end, perhaps all paths lead to fun,
With or without maps, we still come undone.
Laughter is the key, at least that is clear,
No need for directions when joy draws you near.

Paths that Spiral into the Unknown

I took a turn, then thought of a pie,
Each slice of wisdom makes me ask why.
I walked in circles, then waved at a tree,
It waved back, laughing, 'Where's your decree?'

I ran into folks who forgot their own goals,
One flipped a pancake while spinning in shoals.
We held a grand meeting on top of a hill,
To ponder our plans and to grill on a grill.

With every step, I lost a few threads,
My thoughts became noodles, like tangled dread.
'Is that a clue?' said the squirrel with flair,
But I just kept walking, and felt the fresh air.

In spirals we jest, avoiding the humdrum,
The journey, not answers, has kept us all fun.
So paths may twist, and maps may deceive,
We chuckle in circles, still ready to weave.

Distant Dreamscapes and Wayward Souls

A cloud shaped like carrots floated on by,
With outrageous dreams that just made me sigh.
I chased it down, tripped over my shoe,
And laughed at the clouds as I flew with my view.

I met a wise owl who wore funky specs,
He said, 'Life's great, don't become a perplex!'
We danced on rainbows, till they popped like a ball,
And giggled at shadows as we stumbled and sprawled.

A rabbit appeared with a pocket watch drag,
Said, 'Time doesn't matter, don't let it nag!'
We formed a troupe of odd, jolly blokes,
To share in the laughter where life's just a hoax.

So dream on, dear wanderers, let whims take a toll,
For meaning can hide behind laughter's sweet roll.
In distant dreamscapes, we shuffle and sway,
With wayward souls, we shall frolic and play.

The Wanderer's Dilemma

I strolled through a forest of whimsical trees,
Each one whispered secrets, some were mere tease.
I asked a big boulder about life's great cheer,
It rumbled with laughter, saying, 'What's your fear?'

I met a lost gnome, quite puzzled and stuck,
He'd misplaced his hat—had the world run amok?
Together we pondered the ways of our quests,
Spouting nonsensical thoughts like short little jests.

We toyed with the idea of letters and maps,
While giggling at squirrels and their funny mishaps.
'Are we here for wisdom or just for some fun?'
He winked at a raccoon who nodded and run.

So onward we wandered, with a jolly good grin,
Learning that maps can be tangled within.
In the wanderer's dilemma, one truth shines bright,
Sometimes you just laugh, and everything feels right.

Gazing at the Stars

I lifted my gaze towards the night,
Thinking of answers, but lost in flight.
Stars twinkled back with secrets they keep,
I wondered if they too lose sleep.

With a map drawn in lemonade stains,
I scribbled my dreams in runaway trains.
Yet in my quest for a cosmic quest,
I tripped on my shoelaces; what a mess!

The moon winked down, a jester above,
Whispering softly, 'You're not in love.'
With every bright dot, I asked my own fate,
'Do you know where I left my last plate?'

In search of a path, I danced with glee,
Doing the tango with a stray bumblebee.
It buzzed out a tune, but I lost the beat,
Now my left foot's stuck on a chocolate treat.

Missing the Ground

I floated high, like a balloon on the breeze,
Chasing the clouds, convinced I was pleased.
Down below, the grass waved a salute,
But I treated the earth like an old winter boot.

While I aimed for the sun with a hopeful grin,
I forgot I was tangled in my own spin.
Falling, I landed on a pile of fluff,
A cushion of giggles; not quite so tough.

The ground chuckled back as I rolled with grace,
Mud splattered my shoes, it's now a base race.
In my scattered thoughts, I found a new sound,
Life giggles at dreams that float off the ground.

So, I took a break, lounging on air,
With popcorn thoughts tumbling everywhere.
Who needs a road with a pop and a twist?
Sometimes a detour is too good to resist.

The Journey Found in the Questions.

I ventured forth with my heart in tow,
Thoughts like confetti began to grow.
Questions swirled as I took a turn,
Is that a lantern or a nice fry pan burn?

Knocking on doors of curious doubt,
"What's at the end?" is what I'd shout.
With each reply like a mixed-up rhyme,
I lost track of reason, oh, what a time!

The answers danced like playful sprites,
Leading me off on whimsical flights.
But down the road, I tripped on a shoe,
Oh, who knew that confusion could feel so new?

So with a grin, I packed my own doubts,
Turning my musings into cool outs.
For in every question, a riddle can gleam,
And life's just a party; let's all scream!

A Compass Made of Whispers

They said to find north, but how could I know?
My compass spins wild like a door in a show.
With whispers of friends as my only guide,
I wandered the woods with my eyes open wide.

A squirrel passed by with a map in its paws,
I asked for directions; it just laughed and was paused.
"Follow that path where the tall grass waves,"
I swear it was pointing to some hidden caves.

I spun like a top with each turn I took,
Mapless and merry, just a silly old rook.
The trees had their secrets, the birds sang off-key,
But it felt like adventure - just my soul and me.

So I skipped through the woods, with no place to be,
Chasing butterflies, carefree and free.
When lost in my thoughts, the world seemed so grand,
Because whispers and laughter hold more than a plan.

Lost in the Labyrinth of Thought

In a maze of ideas, my mind took a stroll,
Tangled in wonders, losing all control.
Left turns and right turns, where does it end?
A tumble of marbles, no path to defend.

I bumped into logic, wearing a frown,
"Can't you find the way? You're only falling down!"
But I shrugged and smiled, "This wandering's fun,
Even silly detours lead to the sun."

With each twist and turn, I met new delights,
Like candy-floss clouds and glittery nights.
Insults from shadows danced right past me,
"I'm exploring the depths of my own jubilee!"

So lost in my thoughts, I laughed all the more,
For who needs a map when your mind is a store?
The labyrinth's warmth wrapped me like a yarn,
And I spun my own tales, oh what a charm!

The Almanac of Forgotten Dreams

In pockets deep, I store my dreams,
Like socks that vanish, or so it seems.
With a map so vague, it's a wild goose chase,
I trip on thoughts that come with no grace.

Once I had a plan, sharp as a tack,
Now I wander wide, no turning back.
I ask the birds for where to go,
They just chirp and fly, putting on a show.

My compass spins, it twirls and grins,
As I search for purpose in the din.
In jest I laugh, in jest I roam,
A treasure hunt that feels like home.

Through tangled paths of oddities,
I stumble upon quirky curiosities.
With every step, I lose my map,
But oh, what fun, in this silly trap!

Broken Roads and Buried Treasures

The road's a jigsaw, all mixed around,
Each turn a question, no answers found.
I chuckle at signs that lead me astray,
Promising treasures, but where are they, hey?

I once found a pothole, thought it was gold,
Just muddy water, bitter and cold.
With every wrong turn, I shrug and grin,
Perhaps the fun's in the mess I'm in.

A map in my hand, but upside down,
I dance in circles, like a clumsy clown.
Directions? Ha! I prefer to roam,
In this whimsical quest, I've found a home.

So here I wander, with feet so free,
In this chaotic circus, I find my glee.
With treasures buried in laughter and jest,
I trip and tumble, yet feel so blessed!

Reflections in a Pool of Questions

I peer into waters, so murky and dark,
Hoping for answers, just one little spark.
My face in the ripples shows thought and jest,
But why's my reflection wearing a vest?

A question mark dances, it tickles my mind,
The meaning of life, so hard to find.
With ducks all around quacking mysteries,
They seem to know more, oh where are the keys?

I toss in a penny, wish for a clue,
But all that I get is a duck's pooh.
Yet in this confusion, a chuckle I hear,
For the joy of the chase is less about fear.

So I splash in the pool, let laughter arise,
With reflections that beam and surprise.
In questions that swirl, I find my delight,
With giggles aplenty, I'm feeling just right!

The Aurora of Uncertainty

The skies above flicker, oh what a sight,
Colors of doubt swirl in the night.
With a map that's faded and directions askew,
I wonder if aliens might have a clue.

I float on a cloud, pretending to fly,
Chasing my thoughts, which zoom right by.
In this cosmic circus, I giggle and sway,
Lost but delighted in this jolly ballet.

Each star's a riddle, twinkling in jest,
What if life's essence is to love and jest?
With no need for answers, just laughter and cheer,
I twirl with the whirls, embracing my fear.

So here I dance under auroras so bright,
Skipping through constellations, feeling just right.
Lost on the path, but oh what a blast,
In the weight of a giggle, my worries are cast!

The Quest Beyond the Horizon

Onward I march, my shoe laces tied,
With snacks and a drink, but no sense of pride.
Maps are for people who don't like to roam,
I'd rather find treasure in ice cream and foam.

The sun sets low, I ask where I am,
Google Maps chuckles, it's all just a scam.
Pine trees are whispering secrets to me,
But their language is tricky, can't they just be free?

Finding the path feels like driving a car,
Without any fuel, just a shiny guitar.
I strum a few chords, feel the rhythm and rhyme,
Who needs a destination when I'm lost in good time?

So here I shall stay, on this hilltop divine,
With bees and some honey, think I'll be just fine.
Maps may be great, but my heart is the key,
Let's laugh at the chaos, and just let it be!

Voices Lost in the Wilderness

In the woods where the ferns make a soft bed,
I converse with a squirrel, who thinks I'm misled.
He twitches his tail, chats about nuts,
While I ponder life and its many big cuts.

The owls hoot loudly, like they know all the answers,
But all they do is flap and encourage my misadventures.
With moss for a pillow, I nap away dreams,
Of finding my way through the tangle of streams.

"Just follow the river!" a raccoon suggests,
But I keep paddling, accepting these tests.
Tripping on roots, making friends with the flies,
Nature is quirky, you may not be wise!

Yet laughter erupts from my hiccuping chest,
Who needs a clear path when I'm having this fest?
Maps may be boring; they take out the fun,
I'll dance with the trees, 'til I'm one with the sun!

A Labyrinth of Thoughts Unraveled

In a maze of my mind, I spin round and round,
As ideas elude like the lost and the found.
I stutter and mutter, but nothing comes clear,
My thoughts play hide-and-seek, but I have no fear.

A butterfly flutters, whispering hints,
"Life's not a puzzle, just follow the flints."
I chase after shadows, they giggle and tease,
While I figure out why I forgot how to sneeze.

Puppies distract me with their floppy dog ears,
They tumble and bark, reporting my fears.
"Get out of your head!" the wise kitten calls,
Yet, I trip on my thoughts, and trip over walls.

So here I shall frolic in this tangle of woes,
With laughter and wiggles, creativity flows.
Though I'm lost in my thoughts, mischief's my guide,
Maps may be nice, but I'm joyful inside!

Building Bridges in the Space Between

On a bridge made of giggles, I stand all alone,
Constructing some thoughts from the laughter I've sown.
With planks made from chuckles and nails of pure glee,
I traverse to new lands, oh, what wonders to see!

Meanwhile, clouds float by, sharing jokes from above,
I'm twirling and leaping with the hope of a dove.
"This way or that way?!" a sign post would shout,
But I'm more into cartwheels than stressing about route.

My blueprint is scribbles, what could go wrong?
A dash of confusion, and a splash of a song.
Building connections in this whimsical space,
Life's a grand circus, let's all join the race!

So onwards I go, through this zany parade,
With every mad turn, I'm perfectly made.
Who needs a straight path when I've got this flair?
I'll flutter through life, with whimsy to spare!

Raindrops on the Window of Possibility

Raindrops dance on glassy panes,
I forgot my map, where's the train?
My coffee's cold, my mind's a haze,
Lost in thoughts, in a foggy maze.

The streets look shiny, but they're all wrong,
I turned left when I meant to jog.
A squirrel laughs with a nut in hand,
While I wander, lost in this land.

Umbrellas spin like wild top hats,
As puddles splash on pondering cats.
A street sign winks, I blink twice back,
And pretend to find the fun in this track.

So here I sit, with raindrops bright,
In this riddle, I'll find delight.
Adventure's here, though plans may flap,
Oh, look at that! A rubber chap!

Where the Soul Meets the Untraveled

In fields of grass, I wave hello,
To dandelions dancing in the glow.
A GPS won't find my muse,
I'm snagged on thoughts of mismatched shoes.

The compass spins, it's having a blast,
As I shuffle forward, hoping to last.
Chasing shadows beneath the sun,
In this adventure, I'm the only one.

A misplaced sock is the hero today,
With a single shoe leading the way.
I offer a high five to a passing cloud,
Wandering freely, that's how I'm proud.

So let's toast to paths less defined,
With spaghetti maps that mess with the mind.
For every choice, there's laughter in sight,
As I trip through the day and dance with delight.

The Palette of Wandering Emotions

In a gallery where colors collide,
My mood swings dance, nowhere to hide.
With a splash of joy and a stroke of gray,
I mix up laughter in a painted ballet.

Brushes fumble, paint drips on my shoe,
Where's the orange? I just had a clue!
But hey, that green's a funky hue,
Guess it's just me trying to color my view.

Canvases whisper of paths that await,
But I'm busy tripping over fate.
Each misstep is just part of my art,
A masterpiece born from a wandering heart.

So I'll paint with giggles and colors so bright,
Life's just a canvas, let's make it light.
For in every error, a story can sprout,
With a brush of humor, I'll figure it out.

A Clarion Call from the Depths

Deep down under, I hear a voice,
"Where's your map?" It giggles by choice.
Echoes of laughter bounce off the walls,
While I dance with shadows in endless stalls.

I dive for answers, but they all swim,
In circles so wide, they seem quite grim.
"There's treasure here, beneath the fuss,"
Yells a crab in a top hat, full of trust.

With every bubble, I pop a thought,
Beneath the surface, I seek what I sought.
Fishes wink as they slip by fast,
Saying, "Hey buddy, you'll find it at last!"

So here's to the depths, where clowns play the fool,
And maps seem forgotten in a bubbly pool.
For every lost call is a chance to gain,
With giggles and bubbles, I'll dance through the rain.

www.ingramcontent.com/pod-product-compliance
Lightning Source LLC
Chambersburg PA
CBHW071851160426
43209CB00003B/502